T0287172

YORK BUSES SINCE DEREGULATION

KEITH A. JENKINSON

AMBERLEY

First published 2022

Amberley Publishing
The Hill, Stroud
Gloucestershire, GL5 4EP

www.amberley-books.com

Copyright © Keith A. Jenkinson, 2022

The right of Keith A. Jenkinson to be identified
as the Author of this work has been asserted in
accordance with the Copyrights, Designs and
Patents Act 1988.

ISBN 978 1 4456 9704 8 (print)
ISBN 978 1 4456 9705 5 (ebook)

British Library Cataloguing in Publication Data.
A catalogue record for this book is available from
the British Library.

Origination by Amberley Publishing.
Printed in the UK.

Introduction

Founded by the Romans as Eboracum in AD 71, the historic city of York, famous for its medieval architecture and city walls, will never fail to impress its visitors and has much to offer. In addition to its magnificent Gothic cathedral and narrow cobbled streets, it is also home to the National Railway Museum and numerous other attractions, all of which are situated in or close to the city centre. Once served by the trams, trolleybuses and buses operated by the Corporation, in 1934 these were merged with West Yorkshire Road Car Co. into a joint operation under the title York-West Yorkshire Joint Committee, which survived until 10 March 1986, after which the new Citibus fleet name was introduced.

Since deregulation in 1986, much has changed, however, with new independent operators appearing – and disappearing – as well as changes in the ownership of the dominant operator, one of which saw West Yorkshire Road Car Co. sold by the National Bus Company to its management in partnership with East Yorkshire Motor Services chairman Alan Stephenson on 25 August 1987. After adopting the name AJS Holdings Ltd on 27 January 1988, it changed this to AJS Travel Group on 25 January 1989 before becoming Blazefield Travel Group Ltd on 9 October 1991 following Alan Stephenson's withdrawal from the company. West Yorkshire Road Car Co. was not, however, the only former NBC operator whose vehicles were to be seen in York, as East Yorkshire Motor Services, West Riding Automobile Company, and United Automobile Services entered the city from the east, south, and north-west respectively, while independents York Pullman, Reliance Motor Services, Selby-based Jaronda Travel, and G. E. Sykes of Appleton Roebuck also had a minor presence. In addition, two operators provided sightseeing tours of the city: West Yorkshire Road Car Co., having operated one since June 1955, originally using a Bedford OB; and Jorvik Tours of Market Weighton, who began its operations in March 1985 using a Bristol RELH coach and open-top double-deckers. Of the above mentioned independents operating stage carriage services, York Pullman was the oldest, having been founded in 1926, while Reliance had started in 1930 but had been taken over by its current owners in November 1980. Jaronda Travel was, however, much younger, having commenced operation in the 1970s. Then, before deregulation, in January 1985 York Pullman was purchased by John Marsh who changed its name to Reynard Pullman and replaced its classic maroon, cream and yellow livery with a new version using the same three colours, albeit with cream dominating.

The first independent operators to take advantage of deregulation were Glenn Coaches of Wiggington, who started life as a coach company in 1977, Gent Walker of Acaster Malbis; Ingleby's, who operated a service to Stamford Bridge and Pocklington; and Paul Cowell, who began a short-lived service to Poppleton. In the meantime, in October 1986, York Citibus had introduced Ford Transit minibuses to the city, which carryied Hoppa fleet names, while in 1987 the former NBC company replaced the Citibus fleet name on its vehicles, first with West Yorkshire, and then, in April 1988, with York City & District decals.

In 1988, in a bid to manage expected traffic demand up to 2006, York City Council took the decision to create four park & ride sites (increased to five in 1993), the first of which, at

Askham Bar Tesco, was opened in June 1990. A two-year contract to operate the bus service was awarded to Hutchinson's of Husthwaite, who maintained it with coaches adorned with appropriate branding. After proving successful, a second park & ride operation was started, on a cinema car park at Clifton Moor in the run-up to Christmas 1991, but was only available on Saturdays and school holidays until a purpose-built site was opened . The successful bidder for this service, in 1991, was Pocklington-based Jolly Roger, who mainly operated it with coaches but occasionally used one of its double-deck buses. After ceasing trading in July 1993, the Clifton Moor contract was awarded to Glyn Fishwick, and then York Pullman, before later passing to Thornes of Bubwith.

The next newcomers to make an appearance in York were ATL's Leeds-based subsidiary Airebus, which, in 1989, briefly gained a small number of tendered journeys from Leeds; and Premier Buses of Dunnington, who, in November, began competing against York City & District on some city services with a small fleet of new dark-green-and-cream-liveried minibuses carrying the fleet name Target Travel.

1990 proved to be a year of change, starting in February with Reynard Pullman surprisingly selling its coaching unit, the York Pullman name, and twenty coaches to Kingston-upon-Hull City Transport so as to be able to give full concentration to the operation of its local bus services. Following this, a month later AJS Travel Group's York City & District subsidiary sold its open-top sightseeing tour, together with the buses that operated it, to Stratford-upon-Avon-based Guide Friday. Then, on 29 July, AJS Travel Group sold York City & District and Target Travel, which it had purchased in December 1989 but maintained as a separate unit, to employee-owned former West Yorkshire PTE Yorkshire Rider, who at this same time acquired Reynard Pullman. As part of this move, AJS's bus services from Leeds to Whitby, Scarborough, Bridlington, and Hull, the latter two of which were jointly operated with East Yorkshire Motor Services, were, on 2 January, placed under a new AJS Travel Group company, Yorkshire Coastliner. Meanwhile, KHCT-owned York Pullman was the operator chosen by the council to operate its new City Centre Shuttle service, which linked the Barbican coach park with Leeman Road, and used coaches. Another operator to be seen in the city was Ryedale Link, who started operating minibuses on a service to Castle Howard and Malton.

1991 began with York City & District, Target Travel and Reynard Pullman being collectively renamed York City Rider by their new owner, while in August the newly created former AJS Blazefield Travel Group took control of Yorkshire Coastliner, although this was not noticeable to the general public as its livery and identity, etc., remained unchanged. Also in 1991, a new city sightseeing operator made its debut, this being Stadie & Turner who traded under the name Viking Tours with open-top double-deckers from a base at Acaster Airfield. During the following year, in August 1992, Edinburgh-based municipal operator Lothian Region Transport surprisingly entered the York sightseeing market when it acquired a substantial shareholding in Jorvik and transferred some open-top Leyland Atlanteans from the Scottish capital. However, after Jorvik went into receivership in October, it quickly returned north of the border. Then, in December 1992 Viking Tours purchased Jorvik Tours from the receiver, thus increasing its fleet to six buses. In the meantime, after Hutchinson's had lost the Askham Bryan park & ride service to Stevensons of Easingwold in the 1992 retendering process, at the start of 1993 Glyn Fishwick, who had now purchased the Hutchinson business, was successful in gaining the contract to operate the part-time Clifton Moor park & ride service. In addition, a further, park & ride service was planned at Grimston Bar, and while this was being constructed a part-time operation was started at Easter 1992 using York University's Goodricke College car park in Heslington, the contract for which was awarded to local operator Ingleby's Coaches.

Moving forward, in April 1993 Kingston-upon-Hull City Transport sold its twenty-six-vehicle York Pullman operation to Durham Travel Services, who retained the Pullman name. Also operating tours, albeit with coaches, was Eddie Brown of Helperby. With sightseeing being an ever-growing and lucrative market, York Pullman introduced open-top double-deckers, while in May, Lothian Region Transport returned to the city, albeit this time in its own right. Also joining the sightseeing fray during the late summer of 1994 was Yorkshire Belles, whose sole vehicle was a closed-top AEC Routemaster, which it had rebuilt with an open rear staircase to give it a vintage appearance.

In 1995, Rider York took over all the contracts for the city's expanding park & ride services as well as the city centre shuttle, which also served the National Railway Museum. In the meantime, on 15 April 1994 Somerset-based Badgerline had purchased Yorkshire Rider, together with its subsidiary Rider York, before a year later merging with Grampian Region Transport to create FirstBus. Although little changed initially, except for the Yorkshire Rider logo being replaced by that of FirstBus, in 1998 the Rider York fleet name was removed from its buses in favour of a large 'First' logo supplemented with a small 'York' identifier. However, the city suddenly became more colourful, with buses transferred in from other Yorkshire Rider subsidiaries adorned in other styles of its cream and green livery. At around this same time consideration was given to a new colour scheme for the York fleet, which included unrelieved or two-tone green, neither of which proved popular and soon disappeared.

Continuing to expand its park & ride operations, on 5 October 1995 York City Council opened another new site, this time at Grimston Bar, and awarded the contract to Rider York, following this with the opening of a new park & ride site – Rawcliffe Bar – in July 1996.

Meanwhile, also appearing in York towards the end of 1995 was a new form of public transport, a road train, which was operated by the National Railway Museum on a shuttle service between the minster and the museum. Two 'locomotives', each hauling three passenger carriages, were used, initially being lpg-powered, but later converted to diesel fuel.

In November 1997, another new livery appeared in the city when West Riding, which had been purchased from the NBC by Caldaire Holdings in 1987 before being acquired by British Bus in 1995 and then passing to the Cowie Group in August 1996, was rebranded as Arriva, but otherwise unchanged.

In 1998, FirstBus acquired the local bus services of Glenn Coaches, thus further reducing competition in the city. While in November yet another of the city's park & ride sites opened, this being at the McArthurGlen Designer Outlet shopping complex, to which First York provided the bus service with vehicles being painted in a branded livery for the retail park. Also in 1998, a new, albeit small, independent appeared: Bus Force, owned by a Bob Bileckyj, who operated a handful of second-hand minibuses from a base at Acaster Airfield, but never grew in size and ceased trading in the early part of the new millennium. Then, in July 1999, a former Lothian Region Transport director launched a new company in the city under the title Yorkbus using six former Lothian closed-top Leyland Atlanteans. Sadly, however, after proving to be unsuccessful it closed after only four weeks. During the following year, yet another new operator joined the scene, this being Just Travel, who concentrated on the private hire and tours market but also gained a few local school contracts before eventually selling out to York Pullman in January 2018.

Moving forward again and entering the new millennium, February 2000 saw First York purchase Durham Travel Service's York Pullman operations, while in May a Fulford-based newcomer, Top Line Travel, set up in business, gaining the new CitySightseeing franchise in the process. After initially concentrating on its city tour operation, in October Top Line expanded into local bus operation with services to York University. Then, during the following year, a new operator, K&J Logistics, started up in business on the fringe of the city at Rufforth, initially concentrating on private hire work and a few school contracts but, as will be seen later, became a major player in York. Another newcomer to make an appearance in February 2000, and using Acaster Airfield as its base, was Adam Askew, who used York Country Buses and Connexions fleet names and gained a small number of tendered services in and around the city. Although never growing much in size, he continued operating until July 2004, when he admitted defeat and left the scene.

Early in 2002 another new operator to appear in the city was Alan Pearson, who traded as Door to Door and began a small number of local services. Later, in August, strengthening its position in the sightseeing market, Top Line took over Guide Friday's York operation and buses. Following this, on 2 September yet another newcomer to the city made its debut when Harrogate Coach Travel began operating the former United 142 and 143 services from Ripon. Then, on 1 September 2003 it started operating some journeys from York to Selby before adding a service from Askham Bar to Tadcaster on 2 August 2004. This was, however, not the only independent to be seen in the city, as Thornes of Bubwith ran twice each week on a service from Aughton (which it continued until May 2009), while Grimsby-based Amvale maintained an infrequent express (and comparatively short-lived) service from Cleethorpes.

In March 2003, bendibuses made their first appearance into the city when First York transferred nine Volvo B7LAs from Bradford for use on the park & ride services. Meanwhile, another park & ride site was opened on 12 July 2004 at Monks Cross from where First York provided the buses connecting it with the city centre. After proving to be successful, on 8 May 2006 First York introduced twelve more bendibuses to the city, these being new futuristic Wrightbus 'ftr' Volvo B7LA Street Cars painted in a lilac livery, which were placed on the cross-city service from Acomb to the university. Several years later, however, as a consequence of York City Council becoming increasingly unhappy with the 'ftr's, all were withdrawn on 10 March 2012 and transferred to First Leeds for further service.

Yet another new operator attracted to the city was Veolia Transport-owned Dunn Line, who, on 19 February 2007, gained some services in the city that had previously been operated by First York. Using double-deckers and midibuses and sharing Top Line's depot at Fulford, these continued until 31 August 2008 when they were taken over by Transdev Blazefield following its purchase of Veolia's York operation two months after it had acquired Top Line Travel. Then, in October the former Veolia and Top Line operations were combined under the Transdev York identity. Meanwhile, in April 2007, K&J Logistics revived the dormant York Pullman brand, which it then progressively applied to all its buses and coaches, and also started open-top sightseeing tours, which it continued to operate until April 2014.

In January 2009, First York introduced fifteen new Mercedes-Benz O530G bendibuses, painted in a silver livery, on its contracted park & ride services, these replacing the last of the Volvo B7LAs that had been transferred from Bradford in 2003.

In an attempt to gain further expansion, in September 2010 York Pullman began a service from York city centre to the university, which it branded Unilink using several of its buses painted in a dedicated livery. Two years later, however, it sold it along with its other local bus services to Transdev York, who continued to use the Unilink brand until December 2016. Another operator to be seen in York was Dalton-based John Smith & Sons who had, for several years, passed through the city on its 58 service from Thirsk to Northallerton.

On 17 April 2011, Eddie Brown Tours took over the Wetherby to York 412 and 413 services from Arriva, and the Ripon to York 142 and 143 services from Harrogate Coach Travel, although the latter briefly regained them on an emergency contract on 16 December 2014 following Eddie Brown entering receivership and having its licence revoked by the traffic commissioner. On 5 January 2015, however, the 142 and 143 passed to Transdev. Meanwhile, 2011 saw yet another newcomer make an appearance in the city when, on 17 April, Sherburn-in-Elmet independent Utopia gained the contract for the 37 service from York Pullman. Later, however, it lost this to Tockwith-based Sandla Transport Services, who also traded as Arrive-in-Style, but had its licence revoked in November 2013.

A new replacement park & ride site at Askham Bryan and a new one at Poppleton Bar opened in June 2014, the latter being served by new all-electric Optare Versas operated by First York, as too was Monks Cross from May 2015. A month later, on 4 July 2014, a new tours operator appeared in the city when 'The Ghost Bus Tours' began an evening sightseeing operation using two former London Routemasters painted in an all-black livery. Then, in September, a Coastliner York Sightseeing ex-Metrobus, East Lancs-bodied Dennis Trident, gained the honour of being the world's first double-decker to be retrofitted as an all-electric bus. Found to be successful, three of Coastline's other open-top sightseeing double-deckers (ex-Lothian Buses Plaxton-bodied examples) were similarly retrofitted in 2016. Meanwhile, Harrogate Coach Travel, who now used the fleet name Connexions, expanded its presence in the city when it started a new commercially operated local service from Haxby to Copmanthorpe on 2 August 2015 before later expanding with a new service to Acomb.

On 27 March 2016, Yorkshire Coastliner began a new limited-stop express service, branded Cityzap, from York to Leeds, which only took 50 minutes from city to city. Then, later, on 20 September, York TukTuks Ltd made its debut, providing 45-minute tours of the city in six-seat Asian-style vehicles. Unfortunately, however, this proved unsuccessful and ceased operation in the autumn of 2017. Meanwhile, First York trialled an all-electric Optare double-decker, which, being deemed successful, led to an order being placed for twenty-one similar buses for operation on York City Council's park & ride network.

Then, on 19 January 2018, Stephensons of Easingwold suddenly ceased trading, following which its services were taken over by Yorkshire Coastliner, who branded them as York & Country. However, it was York Pullman who acquired the Stephensons name and then, in January 2018, gained further expansion with its takeover of the contracts of local operator Just Travel when it ceased trading. Meanwhile, another operator to appear around the city was A & A Coach Travel, who moved from Boroughbridge to Tockwith from where it continued its private hire and school contract operations with a mixed fleet of single- and double-deckers.

Towards the end of 2019, First York began repainting its Mercedes-Benz bendibuses and all-electric Optare Versas used on the park & ride services into an uninspiring all-blue livery, while in late December the first of its twenty-one all-electric Optare MetroDecker double-deckers began driver training in preparation for their introduction on park & ride duties in March 2020.

With its wide variety of bus operators, liveries, and vehicle types, York never fails to be a fascinating city for the transport enthusiast, and with all its history, architecture, and numerous attractions, is well worthy of a visit.

Still displaying West Yorkshire fleet names, Plaxton dual-purpose-bodied Leyland Leopard 2570 (KUB 544V), which was new in December 1979, is seen here operating a local service in York in 1987. (K. A. Jenkinson)

Seen here opposite York railway station displaying its York West Yorkshire fleet name on its cove panels is ECW-bodied Bristol RELL6G 3328 (LWR 883K), which began life with Keighley West Yorkshire in August 1971. (W. Counter)

New to East Midland in June 1975, ECW-bodied Bristol VRT 1940 (JNU 135N) was acquired by West Yorkshire in March 1982 and is seen here with York City & District logos in 1988, a year before it was sold for scrap. (K. A. Jenkinson)

Wearing unrelieved NBC red livery with York City & District fleet names, Leyland National 2 1520 (SWX 539W), which was new to West Yorkshire in May 1981, is seen here operating a local service. (K. A. Jenkinson)

Having been converted to open-top configuration by West Yorkshire, ECW-bodied Bristol VRT 1954 (DWU 839H), which began life as a conventional double-decker in July 1970, carried a dedicated livery for York's first open-top sightseeing tour. Seen here after transferring to York City & District in November 1987, it served with several other operators before being preserved. (Neil Halliday collection)

New to Thames Valley Traction Co. in March 1965, Bristol FLF6G Lodekka DRX 122C was acquired by Viking Tours, Market Weighton in November 1985 and was later converted by them to open-top configuration before being sold for scrap in July 1994. (Neil Halliday)

Starting life with West Yorkshire in May 1977, Plaxton-bodied Leyland Leopard UWR 772R was later sold to York independent Ingleby's with whom it is seen here on 7 April 1989 operating its service to Stamford Bridge. (K. A. Jenkinson)

New to West Yorkshire in September 1977 and passing to York City & District in November 1987, ECW-bodied Bristol VRT WWR 418S is seen here on 23 November 1989, a month after being sold to Guide Friday for continued use on the York City Tour. (K. A. Jenkinson)

Painted in York City & District's new blue and white livery, largely only applied to its minibuses, is ex-West Yorkshire Leyland National 1478 (RYG 770R), seen here resting at Leeman Road end, York. (M. Counter)

New to West Yorkshire in August 1986 and seen here on Great Hudson Street, York, in August 1990 after being transferred to York City & District, Carlyle-converted Ford Transit 121 (D521 HNW) is being followed by Target Travel Reeve Burgess-bodied Renault S56 G198 NWY. (K. A. Jenkinson)

Heading along Bridge Street, York, on 10 August 1990, is York City & District Robin Hood-bodied Iveco 49.10 163 (E463 TYG), which was new in June 1988. (K. A. Jenkinson)

Local independent Glenn Coaches Duple-bodied Leyland Leopard PJO8T, which was new to City of Oxford in September 1978, awaits its Wigginton and Haxby passengers near York railway station on 2 June 1990. (K. A. Jenkinson)

Purchased new by Reynard Buses in September 1988, Northern Counties-bodied Dodge S56 F851 BUA is seen here on 10 August 1990 opposite York railway station with Reynard Pullman lettering on its bonnet and Yorbus on its side panels. (K. A. Jenkinson)

Making its way along George Hudson Street, York, on 2 June 1990 is all-white-liveried York City & District ECW-bodied Leyland Olympian 90 (B90 SWX), which was new to West Yorkshire in September 1984 numbered 1843. (K. A. Jenkinson)

Seen opposite York railway station on 10 August 1990 is Yorkshire Rider ex-Target Travel Reeve Burgess-bodied Renault S56 G195NWY still in the livery of its original owner. Following behind are two of York City Bus, now also Yorkshire Rider, Carlyle-converted Ford Transits sporting Hoppa fleet names. (K. A. Jenkinson)

Awaiting its passengers on local service 14 to Elmfield Avenue is Reynard Pullman Duple-bodied Bedford YMQ FCY 286W, which was new to South Wales Transport in November 1980. (K. A. Jenkinson)

Heading past York railway station on 10 August 1990 en route to South Bank is Yorkshire Rider's Northern Counties-bodied Renault S56 E166 CNC, which was new to Fylde Borough Transport in June 1988. Here it is seen still wearing the livery of Reynard Bus whose business had been purchased by Rider two weeks earlier. (K. A. Jenkinson)

Still wearing the livery of West Yorkshire, from whom it had been transferred, is York City & District Leyland Lynx 7 (F207 MBT), seen here on Station Road, York, on 2 June 1990. (K. A. Jenkinson)

Heading through the centre of York on a journey from Scarborough and wearing National Express corporate livery is West Yorkshire Plaxton Supreme V-bodied Leyland Leopard 2589 (GWU 561T), which dated from May 1979. (K. A. Jenkinson)

Displaying a Citybus fleet name and the remains of an NBC logo, ECW-bodied Leyland Olympian 1832 (A683 MWX), which was new to York West Yorkshire in February 1984, is seen here operating a city service to Burton Stone Lane. (W. Counter)

Leaving York railway station at the start of its journey to Castle Howard and Malton on 2 June 1990 is Ryedale Link's Dormobile-bodied Ford Transit, which later passed to Halifax independent T. J. Walsh, who re-registered it TJI9143. (K. A. Jenkinson)

En route from Bridlington to Leeds, Yorkshire Coastliner Plaxton-bodied Leyland Leopard 466 (KUB 666V), which was new to West Yorkshire in January 1980, collects its passengers opposite York station on 10 August 1990. (K. A. Jenkinson)

New to Bailey, Fangfoss, in December 1978, but seen here on 10 August 1990 after being acquired by Glyn Fishwick, Plaxton-bodied Ford R1114 OVY 203T passes York railway station on its York City Council park & ride journey to Askham Bar, for which it is suitably branded. (K. A. Jenkinson)

In 1991, Yorkshire Rider repainted ex-West Yorkshire ECW-bodied Leyland Olympian 5195 (A599 NYG) into a proposed new livery for its York City Rider operations. This, however, was immediately disliked and thus 5195 never left the paint shop in these colours and was, instead, quickly repainted into Rider's cream and green. (Neil Halliday collection)

New to Barrow Corporation in July 1987 and later passing to Stagecoach, Reeve Burgess-bodied Renault S56 E779 DEO, still in its previous owner's livery, is seen here in York on 2 June 1990 soon after being acquired by Reynard Pullman. (K. A. Jenkinson)

Seen in York on 10 August 1990 when only two months old, Alexander-bodied Leyland Olympian 5207 (G607 OWR) carries both York City & District and Yorkshire Rider fleet names as it turns into Great Hudson Street en route to Acomb Park. (K. A. Jenkinson)

Making its way along Station Road, York, soon after starting its journey to Ripon on 10 August 1990, is United's ECW-bodied Bristol VRT 828 (PAJ 828X) which was then nine years old. (K. A. Jenkinson)

Seen earlier in this book in closed-top form, after being converted to open-top configuration Jorvik Tours ex-Thames Valley Bristol FLF6G Lodekka DRX 122C awaits custom near York railway station while operating a city tour. (Author's collection)

Making its way along Rougier Street, York, in 1990 while operating the City Centre Shuttle service, for which it is branded, is York Pullman PKU 78X, a Plaxton-bodied Bedford YNT, which started life with N&S, Elsecar, in May 1982. (Neil Halliday collection)

New to Harrogate & District four months earlier, Reeve Burgess-bodied Renault S75 G295 MWU is seen here in York on 10 August 1990 after being transferred to Yorkshire Coastliner into whose livery it has been repainted. (K. A. Jenkinson)

Immaculately presented after being repainted into Yorkshire Rider's corporate livery and given two fleet names, ECW-bodied Bristol VRT 743 (LWU 471V), which started life with York West Yorkshire in May 1980, turns into Great Hudson Street on 10 August 1990. (K. A. Jenkinson)

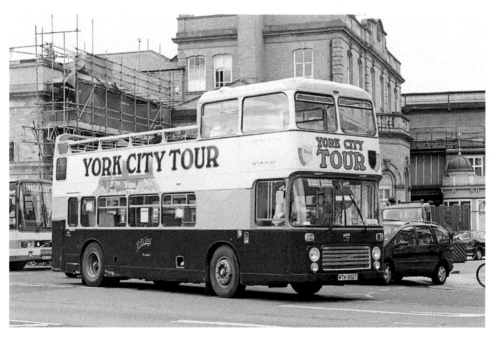

Seen at York railway station is Viking Tours open-top ECW-bodied Bristol VRT WTH 962T which started life in April 1979 with South Wales Transport as a conventional closed-top bus. (Author's collection)

Hiding its owner's identity as it stands at its terminus in Rougier Street, York, before returning to its home town, is Harrogate & District ECW-bodied Leyland Olympian 391 (C482 YWY), which when new in November 1985 was numbered 1860 in the West Yorkshire fleet. (K. A. Jenkinson)

Operating the York City Council park & ride service to Clifton Moor in May 1992 is independent Jolly Roger's immaculately presented Plaxton-bodied Bedford YNT GBO 244W, which started life in Wales with Hill, Tredegar, in March 1981. (Author's collection)

Painted in park & ride livery with its owner's, Stephensons Nationwide Travel, name displayed in a side window, former Northern General Willowbrook-bodied Leyland Leopard TUP 585V, which was new in January 1980, is seen here operating York City Council's White Line service on 19 November 1992. (K. A. Jenkinson)

Passengers are seen here boarding Gent-Walker's fare box-fitted ex-Ribble Marshall-bodied Leyland Leopard DRN 664D at Leeman Gardens prior to its departure on its local service to Acomb. (K. A. Jenkinson)

New to West Yorkshire in December 1976 numbered 1477, and passing to Yorkshire Rider in 1979, Leyland National RYG 769R is seen here on loan to Rider York from Yorkshire Rider Leeds, whose identifier is seen alongside its fleet name. (K. A. Jenkinson)

Seen in Coppergate, York, on 16 August 1994 is Yorkshire Coastliner 401 (F401 XWR), an Optare-bodied Mercedes-Benz 811D, which began life with Welwyn Hatfield Line in August 1988. (K. A. Jenkinson)

Resting at its base at Acaster airfield on 25 April 1998 branded for the York City Tour, Jorvik Viking Tours open-top Metro Cammell-bodied Leyland PDR1/1 Atlantean WJY 758 began life with Plymouth City Transport in September 1962 as a conventional closed-top bus. (K. A. Jenkinson)

On the same day, 16 August 1994, another of Viking Tours' York City Tour open-toppers, this time MDS 687P, a former Glasgow PTE Alexander-bodied Leyland Atlantean, is seen in operation. (K. A. Jenkinson)

Delivered new to Yelloway, Rochdale, in 1986, Neoplan Skyliner RIB 4313 is seen here in corporate National Express livery with Durham Transport Services about to pass under York's city walls. (K. A. Jenkinson)

Kingston-upon-Hull City Transport open-top Roe-bodied Leyland Atlantean 195 (NAT 341M), which dated from November 1973, is seen here at the Barbican, York, on 16 August 1994 wearing York Pullman City Tour livery. (K. A. Jenkinson)

Unsure as to where it is going, Yorkshire Coastliner's two-year-old Northern Counties-bodied Leyland Olympian 402 (K2YCL), seen here at York railway station on 16 August 1994, shows 845 Bridlington-Filey on its destination screen but carries a handwritten Whitby label in its windscreen. (K. A. Jenkinson)

Seen again, this time on 16 August 1994 operating York City Council's Green Line park & ride service to Clifton Moor, for which it carries branding on its side panel, is York Pullman Plaxton-bodied Bedford YNT PKU 78X. (K. A. Jenkinson)

Seen at York railway station on 16 August 1994, en route to Scarborough on the X95 service, is Harrogate & District Leyland National 2 UWX 70X, which was new to West Yorkshire in September 1981. (K. A. Jenkinson)

Rider York's ex-Target Travel Reeve Burgess-bodied Renault S56 G253 LWF, with a Flagship label in its windscreen and a side window, is pictured here at York railway station on 16 August 1994. (K. A. Jenkinson)

Wearing the livery of its previous owner, Harrogate Independent Travel, but new to Lucketts, Watford, in October 1989, is Harrogate & District Wadham Stringer-bodied Leyland Swift 205 (G112 VMM), seen here in Rougier Street, York, preparing for its return trip to Harrogate on 30 August 1994. (K. A. Jenkinson)

New in March 1974 to Eastern Counties, ECW-bodied Bristol VRT RAH 132M then served with Cambus, Luton & District, and Bee Line, before being acquired by independent Sykes, Appleton Roebuck, in October 1993. Seen here resting between school duties near the river in York on 20 August 1994, it was sold to Stephensons, Easingwold, in 1998 and after its withdrawal two years later, became a store shed until ultimately being scrapped. (K. A. Jenkinson)

Pictured here on 16 August 1994 is Rider York's much-travelled Duple-bodied Volvo B58 1461 (JSJ4 29W), which was new to A1 Service, Ardrossan, in March 1981 and then served with Rhodes Coaches, Yeadon, whose business was taken over by Yorkshire Rider earlier in 1994. (K. A. Jenkinson)

Starting life with South Wales Transport in December 1979 registered CCY 818V is Bubwith-based Thornes re-registered Leyland National 2 BBT 380V, with Independent fleet name. It is seen here in August 1995 operating the York City Council park & ride service to Clifton Moor. (Author's collection)

Resting between school duties in York on 27 June 1994 is York Pullman Roe-bodied Leyland Atlantean 186 (NAT 345M), which still displays the identity of Pullman's owner, Kingston-upon-Hull City Transport. (K. A. Jenkinson)

Transferred to Harrogate & District from West Yorkshire, to whom it was new in April 1990, Leyland Lynx 382 (G382 MWU) is seen here in Station Rise, York, operating the long X50 service to Skipton, a distance of 50 miles. (K. A. Jenkinson)

Rider York Duple-bodied Leyland Leopard 1553 (UWY 86X), which started life with West Yorkshire painted in NBC white livery in August 1981, climbs Station Rise, York, on the local 10A service to Copmanthorpe on 18 August 1994. (K. A. Jenkinson)

Another former West Yorkshire bus, seen here at York railway station, is Rider York ECW-bodied Bristol VRT 977 (SWW 302R), which dates from December 1976. After passing to First Eastern National in January 1995, it was sold for scrap in December 1997. (K. A. Jenkinson)

York independent Glenn Coaches former National Welsh 1978 vintage Leyland National WUH 172T looks immaculate as it climbs Station Rise while operating a local service from its home base at Wigginton. (K. A. Jenkinson)

New to Yorkshire Rider's Bradford depot in September 1987, Optare StarRider-bodied Mercedes-Benz 811D 2001 (E201 PWY) is seen here in its new home city after being transferred to Rider York. (K. A. Jenkinson)

Optare Delta-bodied DAF SB220 1251 (G251 JYG), which dated from December 1989, was transferred, together with some of its sisters, to Rider York from Yorkshire Rider Leeds. (K. A. Jenkinson)

En Route to Bishopthorpe displaying Rider York livery and fleet names is Leyland National 2 1352 (UWY 74X), which started life with West Yorkshire in November 1981 numbered 1532. (K. A. Jenkinson)

Both JKW 215W, which was new to South Yorkshire PTE in February 1981, and ABR 869S, which began life with United in September 1977, originally carried Duple coach bodies. When purchased by Reynard Buses in November 1990, both these Leyland Leopards were given new Plaxton bodies and are seen here with Rider York, after its purchase of Reynard, operating the City Centre Shuttle on 16 August 1994. (K. A. Jenkinson)

Collecting its passengers outside York Barbican coach park on 16 August 1994 is Eddie Brown's Van Hool-bodied Leyland Tiger AAL551A, which additionally carries York Tour lettering. (K. A. Jenkinson)

Leaving York railway station on 16 August 1994 while undertaking a British Rail York Charter is Paul's Coaches' nineteen-year-old Duple-bodied Bedford YRT KVL 78P. (K. A. Jenkinson)

Climbing Station Rise, York, on a journey from Scarborough to Leeds is Yorkahire Coastliner 405 (L9 YCL), an Alexander-bodied Volvo Olympian that first entered service in May 1994. (K. A. Jenkinson)

Painted in heritage livery with York West Yorkshire and Rider York fleet names is Leyland National 2 363 (PNW 603W), which was new to West Yorkshire in August 1980 with fleet number 1510. (K. A. Jenkinson)

Recreating the old York Corporation livery, Rider York's ECW-bodied Leyland Olympian 5196 (A600 NYG), which began life with West Yorkshire in June 1984 numbered 1837, prepares to pass under the city's historic wall at the top of Station Rise on 5 October 1995. (K. A. Jenkinson)

Turning into Askham Bar park & ride site on 5 October 1995 when only a few weeks old, Rider York Wrightbus-bodied Scania L113 CRL 8417 (N417 ENW) is seen here adorned with park & ride and Flagship branding. (K. A. Jenkinson)

Awaiting its departure from Piccadilly, York, at the start of its journey to Selby and Cawood on 5 October 1995 is Jaronda Travel Plaxton-bodied Dennis Dart K601HWR, which was purchased new by the company in December 1992. (K. A. Jenkinson)

Seen at York railway station on the 57 service to Helmsley on 6 October 1995 is Stephenson of Easingwold's EGR 707S, a Plaxton-bodied Leyland Leopard that began life with Northern General in May 1978. (K. A. Jenkinson)

Resting on Knavesmire Road, alongside York racecourse, is Stephenson of Easingwold's ECW-bodied Leyland Olympian JTY 399X, which had also begun life on Tyneside with Northern General in December 1981. (K. A. Jenkinson)

Awaiting custom near York railway station on 5 October 1995 is Jorvik Tours' twenty-one-year-old, open-top, Park Royal-bodied Leyland Atlantean RCN 106N, which had started life with Gateshead & District as a conventional closed-top bus. (K. A. Jenkinson)

New to London Transport in June 1960 registered WLT 388, and later operated by Kelvin Scottish who re-registered it EDS 300A, Routemaster RM388 was acquired by Yorkshire Belles, Haxby, in May 1994. After conversion to rear open-staircase layout for York sightseeing duties, it is seen here in the city on 5 October 1995. (K. A. Jenkinson)

Heading along Station Road, York, on the 79 service to Harrogate on 16 March 1998 is Harrogate & District Alexander-bodied Volvo B6 664 (M384 VWX). (K. A. Jenkinson)

Starting life in June 1995 with Greater Manchester North before passing to First Huddersfield, Northern Counties-bodied Dennis Dart 3299 (M615 SBA) is seen here on 16 March 1998, still in its previous operator's livery, after being transferred to Rider York. (K. A. Jenkinson)

Seen climbing Station Rise, York, on 16 March 1998 is Durham Travel Services Plaxton-bodied Dennis Dart SLF R120 FUP, which was new in November 1997 and wears Pullman Eastlink branding. In 2000 it passed to Rider York and was numbered 3379 before becoming 32630 in First's national numbering scheme. (K. A. Jenkinson)

Also seen on Station Rise on 16 March 1998 is Rider York Plaxton-bodied Dennis Dart SLF 3302 (P302 AUM), which dated from April 1997 and is painted in FirstBus Quality Service livery. (K. A. Jenkinson)

Standing in the gateway of its owner Sykes' Appleton Roebuck premises on 25 April 1998 is Van Hool-bodied Volvo B10M BAZ 7053, which began life with Shearings in February 1990 registered G853 RNC. (K. A. Jenkinson)

Both new to Ribble in 1976, ECW-bodied Leyland Atlanteans RFR 418P and SFV 425P are seen here at Durham Travel Services, Elvington, York, depot on 24 April 1998 with York Pullman fleet names on the livery of their former operator, OK Motor Services. (K. A. Jenkinson)

Also seen at the Elvington premises of Durham Travel Services on 24 April 1998, with York Pullman fleet name, is Alexander-bodied Leyland Atlantean AVK 179V, which started life with Tyne & Wear PTE in August 1980. (K. A. Jenkinson)

New to Eastern National, but acquired by Durham Travel Services from Sovereign, Leyland National WJN 558S stands alongside Plaxton-bodied Volvo B10M H35CNL, which was new to DTS in February 1990. Both vehicles carry York Pullman fleet names as they rest at its Elvington depot on 24 April 1998. (K. A. Jenkinson)

Seen at the Sutton on the Forest depot of Reliance Motor Services on 25 April 1998 are ex-Lancaster City Transport East Lancs-bodied Leyland Atlantean TCK 200X, which dates from July 1982, and Optare Delta-bodied DAF SB220 R26 GNW, which was purchased new in September 1997. (K. A. Jenkinson)

An unusual vehicle operated by Reliance was Elme-bodied Leyland Swift F992 BFR, which was new to Liddell, Auchinleck, in April 1989 and is seen here at its new owner's depot on 25 April 1998. (K. A. Jenkinson)

Resting in the yard of Reliance Motor Services on 25 April 1998 is Alexander-bodied Leyland Leopard OSJ 614R, which was new to Western SMT in December 1976 and had been purchased from Robson, Thornaby, to provide a source of spares. (K. A. Jenkinson)

Wearing an unrelieved red livery and originally intended for First Glasgow, Rider York Plaxton-bodied Dennis Dart SLF 3323 (P836 YUM), which started life in July 1997, heads into the city on 25 April 1998. (K. A. Jenkinson)

East Yorkshire's full height ECW-bodied Bristol VRT 501 (JKH 501V) is seen opposite York railway station at the end of its journey from Hull on the 746 service. (Rob McCaffery)

Seen near York railway station operating its city tour in July 1994 is Lothian Region Transport open-top Alexander-bodied Leyland Atlantean 925 (OFS 925M), which dated from February 1974 and had been converted to open-top and single-door layout. (K. A. Jenkinson)

Entering York on the 405 service from Selby, West Riding ECW-bodied Leyland Olympian 510 (CWR 510Y) is seen in its immediate post-NBC livery with West Riding Selby fleet name. New in October 1982, it ended its life in 2005 with Rapsons Highland Scottish. (K. A. Jenkinson)

Branded for the Green Line park & ride service, but seen here in St Leonards Place, York, operating route 12 to Haxby and Wiggington, is Rider York Ikarus-bodied DAF SB220 1201 (J422 NCP), which was new in July 1992. (K. A. Jenkinson)

Climbing Station Rise, and painted in park & ride livery, is First York Wright Axcess Ultra Low-bodied Scania L113CRL 8410 (N410 ENW), which was new in September 1995 and later passed to First Midland Bluebird in Scotland. (K. A. Jenkinson)

Rider York's freshly repainted Leyland National 2 1343 (MNW 130V), which began life with West Yorkshire in May 1980, awaits its passengers opposite York railway station. (K. A. Jenkinson)

New to Shamrock & Rambler in October 1987, Carlyle-bodied Freight Rover 374D E235 NFX is seen here at the Acaster Malbis premises of its new owner, York independent Bus Force, on 25 April 1998. (K. A. Jenkinson)

Painted in an unrelieved green livery, First York's Roe-bodied Leyland Atlantean 6234 (PUA 324W), which began life with West Yorkshire PTE in July 1981, is seen here outside York railway station. (Author's collection)

Still wearing the livery of its previous owner, First Huddersfield, and seen here in Station Rise, York, is Rider York Plaxton-bodied Mercedes-Benz 709D 2231 (M231 VWU), which was new in May 1995. (K. A. Jenkinson)

New to York West Yorkshire in February 1984 and now wearing First York livery, ECW-bodied Leyland Olympian 5194 (A686 MWX) is about to pass under the city wall at the top of Station Rise on 3 August 1989. (K. A. Jenkinson)

Seen climbing Station Rise, York, on 3 August 1999 en route to the National Railway Museum is one of its road trains, N923 EOR, which operates a connecting service from the Minster. (K. A. Jenkinson)

Starting life with Greater Manchester North in June 1995 and later operating with First Huddersfield, seen here with First York on 3 August 1999 wearing an unrelieved green livery, is Northern Counties-bodied Dennis Dart 3300 (M616 SBA). (K. A. Jenkinson)

With York Minster forming the backdrop, First York Alexander-bodied Dennis Dart SLF 3365 (T365 NUA) is seen on Station Rise on 3 August 1999, when less than a month old. (K. A. Jenkinson)

New to West Yorkshire in May 1983, First York ECW-bodied Leyland Olympian 5187 (FUM 487Y) is seen here painted in an all-over advertising livery for York Dungeon. (K. A. Jenkinson)

Resting at the short-lived Yorkbus's depot on 3 August 1999 are two ex-Lothian Alexander-bodied Leyland Atlanteans headed by GSC 656X, which was new in October 1981. (K. A. Jenkinson)

Branded for cross-city route 7 and displaying 'super low floor' lettering on its door, First York Plaxton-bodied Dennis Dart SLF 3303 (P303 AUM) is seen here heading up Station Rise on 3 August 1999. (K. A. Jenkinson)

Also seen on Station Rise on 3 August 1999 is First York Plaxton-bodied Dennis Dart SLF 3313 (P826 YUM), which wears a branded livery for the Designerline 99 service. (K. A. Jenkinson)

Seen in June 2002 operating the York City Connexions route C3 is independent Door to Door's Tricentrol-derived Plaxton Paramount-bodied Bedford YMP LUI 3024. (LowlanderLR3)

Purchased new by Adam Askew in February 2000, Plaxton Beaver-bodied Mercedes-Benz 0814 V91 UVY is seen here at Colton sporting York Country Buses and Connexions fleet names when only two months old. (LowlanderLR3)

Painted in Yorkshire Coastliner livery, coach-seated ECW-bodied Leyland Olympian 1857 (C479 YWY) rests in Rougier Street, York, with sister 1833, behind, in an all-over advert for Picher Homes. (K. A. Jenkinson)

Yet another ECW-bodied Leyland Olympian to be seen in York was Harrogate & District 314 (B514 UWW), seen here on 3 August 1999 climbing Station Rise at the start of its journey on the 79 service to Harrogate. (K. A. Jenkinson)

Twenty-one-year-old MCW Metrobus BYX115V, which began life as a conventional closed-top bus with London Transport, is seen here circumnavigating Walmgate Bar on 27 August 2000, operating a sightseeing tour for Top Deck Travel, after being converted to open-top configuration. (K. A. Jenkinson)

Squeezing past an open-top sightseeing MCW Metrobus in Tower Street on 28 August 2000 is First York's ex-West Yorkshire ECW-bodied Leyland Olympian 5189 (FUM 492Y) painted in the short-lived two-tone green livery. (K. A. Jenkinson)

Seen in 2006 while on loan to First York is Hispano-bodied Volvo B7L demonstrator BX03OVZ, which was new in July 2003. (Tommy Holland collection)

Purchased new in March 1987 registered D192 HDE, but seen here on 9 July 2004 owned by Charter Coach, Tockwith, is Duple 340-bodied DAF SB2300 115CUF. (K. A. Jenkinson)

Transferred to First York from First Bradford, to whom it was new in July 2000, Wright Fusion-bodied Volvo B7LA bendibus 10042 (W129 DWX) is seen here on 30 March 2007 wearing park & ride branding. (R. G. Pope)

Wearing its original livery and still fitted with front wheel covers, First York Wrightbus ftr-bodied Volvo B7LA StreetCar 19011 (YK06 AUC) approaches the bus stop opposite York railway station on 30 March 2007. (R. G. Pope)

New to London Buses in closed-top form in June 1984, and later operated by Stagecoach Fife and Redby, Sunderland, from whom it was purchased by York Pullman, all-Leyland Titan A613THV, now an open-topper, is seen here on Tower Street operating a city tour on 8 August 2008. (K. A. Jenkinson)

Seen at Askham Bar on 8 August 2008 is Harrogate Coach Travel's former Burnley & Pendle Alexander-bodied Mercedes-Benz 811D H70 CFV, which was new in April 1991. (K. A. Jenkinson)

Resting in the yard of York Pullman's depot on 8 August 2008 is ex-Arriva Merseyside Northern Counties-bodied Leyland Olympian F255 YTJ painted in Studentlink livery. (K. A. Jenkinson)

Sporting K & J Travel fleet names is York Pullman's Plaxton-bodied Volvo B10M MIW 5792, seen here at its owner's depot on 8 August 2008. (K. A. Jenkinson)

With its destination blind already reset for its return journey to Selby, Arriva Yorkshire's 2000 vintage Wright Renown-bodied Volvo B10BLE 106 (W106 EWU) arrives in Piccadilly, York, on 8 August 2008. (K. A. Jenkinson)

Originally registered N631XBU by Bullock, Cheadle, when new in November 1995, Harrogate Coach Travel's Wright Ultra Low-bodied Scania L113CRL, re-registered EIG 1356, makes its way along Rougier Street, York, on 8 August 2008. (K. A. Jenkinson)

All-Leyland Olympian J113 KCW, which was new to Preston Bus in March 1992, is seen here passing York railway station in March 2011 painted in York Pullman's Unibus livery. (Rob McCaffery)

Branded for the X54 service from Harrogate, and seen here travelling along Piccadilly, York, on 8 August 2008, is Harrogate & District Wright Eclipse Urban-bodied Volvo B7RLE 451 (YJ05 FNK). (K. A. Jenkinson)

Also seen in Piccadilly, York, on 8 August 2008 on the 181 service from Malton, is Stephenson of Easingwold's ten-year-old ex-Arriva Kent & Surrey Plaxton-bodied Mercedes-Benz 0814 2701 (R112 TKO). (K. A. Jenkinson)

New to Burnley & Pendle in July 2001, Wright-bodied Volvo B10BLE 1064 (Y164 HRN) is seen here in its new home city in March 2011 after being transferred to Transdev York and repainted into its blue livery. (Rob McCaffery)

Adorned with branding for Claret Line route 10, First York Wright Eclipse Metro-bodied Volvo B7L 60900 (YJ51 RFN), which was new in February 2002, collects some passengers in Piccadilly, York, on 8 August 2008. (K. A. Jenkinson)

Seen departing from Monks Cross shopping complex, York, on 8 August 2008, is First York Wright Crusader-bodied Volvo B6BLE 40578 (YJ51 RHU), which by then was seven years old. (K. A. Jenkinson)

Also leaving Monks Cross shopping centre on 8 August 2008 is Dunn Line's Veolia-liveried East Lancs-bodied MAN 14.220 ML53 BLU, which had started life with Bluebird, Middleton, in September 2003. (K. A. Jenkinson)

With not much further to go to the York railway station terminus of the X46 service from Hull, for which it carries branding, is East Yorkshire Wright Eclipse Gemini 2-bodied Volvo B9TL 743 (YX08 FXE), seen here on 10 August 2008. (K. A. Jenkinson)

With York Minster in the background, Arriva Yorkshire West's Wetherby-bound Alexander-bodied Dennis Dart SLF 166 (W166 HBT) passes First York Wright Eclipse Urban-bodied Volvo B7RLE 69003 (YK54 ENN), which is collecting passengers in Station Rise on 10 August 2008. (K. A. Jenkinson)

Also seen on Station Rise, York, on 10 August 2008, is First York Wright Eclipse Metro-bodied Volvo B7L 60921 (YG02 DLN), which wears the then current park & ride livery. (K. A. Jenkinson)

Top Line Travel's ex-Metrobus East Lancs-bodied Dennis Trident T407 SMV, which was new in August 1999 as a conventional closed-top bus, is seen here at Leeman Gardens, York, nine years later, after being converted to part open-top and painted in City Sightseeing livery. (K. A. Jenkinson)

Wearing the then latest version of York's park & ride livery, First York Wright Eclipse Urban-bodied Volvo B7RLE 69378 (YJ08 XYT) was only a few days old when seen in Rougier Street on 8 August 2008. (K. A. Jenkinson)

Climbing Station Rise, York, on 8 August 2008 on its way from Whitby to Leeds, is Transdev Yorkshire Coastliner Wright Eclipse Gemini 2-bodied Volvo B9TL 412 (FJ08 BYK), which was new in March 2008. (K. A. Jenkinson)

Supplied new to Delgro, Singapore, in December 1994, but repatriated to Metroline (London) in August 2000, Alexander Royale-bodied Volvo Olympian M650 ELA was originally in dual-door format. After being converted to single-door layout, it is seen in Station Rise, York, on 8 August 2008 operated by Dunn Line in Veolia livery on the 14 service to Clifton. A few days later it was transferred to Veolia Cymru before ultimately being scrapped in August 2012. (K. A. Jenkinson)

Both new to First York in 2001/2, Alexander-bodied Volvo B7TL 30964 (YJ51 RAU) passes Wright Crusader-bodied Volvo B6BLE 40587 (YJ51 RFZ) on Station Rise, York, on 10 August 2008. (K. A. Jenkinson)

Arriva Yorkshire West's seven-year-old Plaxton-bodied Volvo B7TL 681 (X681 YUG) collects its Selby-bound passengers at the terminus of its 415 service in Piccadilly, York, in August 2008. (K. A. Jenkinson)

Freshly repainted, York Pullman Alexander-bodied Volvo Olympian M205 VSX, which was new to Lothian in April 1995, is seen here opposite York railway station on 24 November 2011 while operating a service to the city's university. (Murdoch Currie)

Originally a BMC demonstrator when new in September 2007, BMC 220 BV57 MPU is seen here in York in March 2011 after being purchased by York Pullman. (Rob McCaffery)

Still wearing its Veolia-Dunn Line livery, Optare Solo 1265 (YJ56 WUV) is seen here in York after being purchased, along with its previous owner's operations, by Transdev whose identity has been applied. (Rob McCaffery)

Carrying route branding for the Leeds–York service in March 2011 is Transdev Yorkshire Coastliner Optare Versa 273 (YJ57 XWW), which started life with Lancashire United in February 2008. (Rob McCaffery)

New in August 2015 as a demonstrator for its chassis manufacturer, Wright-bodied Volvo B8RLE BA15 BXS is seen here in York at the start of its journey to Easingwold on 22 May 2016 after being purchased by Reliance, Sutton on the Forest. (Author's collection)

Starting life with Chester City Transport in January 2004, BMC-bodied BMC 1100 BU53 PNO is seen here operating for Sandla Transport Services who used the fleet name Arrive-in-Style. (T. M. Leach collection)

Twenty-three-seat slimline Optare Solo MB07BUS, which began life with Mott, Aylesbury, in May 2007, is seen here in York while operating for Sherburn-in-Elmet independent Utopia Coaches. (T. M. Leach collection)

Painted in Unibus livery is Transdev York Plaxton-bodied Volvo B7TL 2717 (PL51 LDX), which had been acquired from Go-Ahead London General to whom it was new in February 2002. (D. W. Rhodes)

Painted in Reliance, Sutton on the Forest's traditional livery, Wright-bodied Volvo B7RLE YJ09PBF, which had been purchased new by its operator in May 2009, is seen here in St Leonards Place, York, followed by First York Alexander-bodied Volvo B7TL 30955 (YJ51 RCU). (D. W. Rhodes)

Departing from Exhibition Square, York, at the start of its journey to Helmsley is Stephenson of Easingwold's Alexander Dennis Enviro300 SN06BSV, which was new to its owner in June 2006. (D. W. Rhodes)

Heading along George Hudson Street, York, Transdev York's Unibus-liveried Alexander Dennis Enviro200-bodied MAN 14.240 1107 (YJ60 ADU) started life with York Pullman in September 2010. (D. W. Rhodes)

Seen here is one of the little vehicles that were briefly operated by YorkTukTuks on sightseeing tours around the city. (YorkTukTuks)

Wearing Little Explorers livery, Transdev York Transbus Dart SLF 706 (YJ04 LXN), which was new to Keighley & District in March 2004, heads through a York suburb on its way to Easingwold on 7 April 2018. (Author's collection)

Still wearing the livery of its previous owner, Burnley & Pendle to whom it was new in April 2012, Optare Versa 216 (YJ12 MZZ) is seen here in York on 12 November 2018 shortly after its transfer to Transdev York. (Richard Walter)

Harrogate Coach Company (Connexions) Optare Tempo YJ56 ATU, which was new to Tanat Valley in October 2006, is seen here in Station Road, York, on 12 November 2018 still painted in the livery of its previous owner, Norfolk Green. (Richard Walter)

Seen at dusk on 12 November 2018 with a fixed York Races Shuttle destination display is York Pullman's Wright-bodied Volvo B7TL TJZ4 286, which was new to Go-Ahead London General in October 2002 registered LF52 ZRX. (Richard Walter)

Sporting an all-over livery to promote its operator's tap and go app, Transdev York's Alexander-bodied Dennis Dart SLF Little Explorer 703 (YG52 GDJ), which started life with Harrogate & District in November 2002, is seen here in Station Road, York, on 12 November 2018. (Richard Walter)

Painted in Transdev's generic Pride of the North livery is Yorkshire Coastliner's Wright Eclipse Gemini 2-bodied Volvo B9TL 421 (BD11CEA), seen here in Station Road, York, operating the CityZap service to Leeds on 12 November 2018. (Richard Walter)

New to Reliance, Sutton on the Forest, in September 2018, Alexander Dennis E20 YX68 URM) heads along Station Road, York, when only two months old. (Richard Walter)

On loan from distributors Pelican Engineering to First York, who gave it temporary fleet number 62990, all-electric Yutong E12LF demonstrator YK66 CBC, which was new in February 2017, is seen here in service at the top of Station Rise in January 2018. (Scott Poole)

Arriva Yorkshire's Optare Solo 3020 (YJ08 XBF), seen here on Station Road, York, 12 November 2018, started life with Arriva Durham County in September 2008. (Richard Walter)

Local operator Just Travel's Van Hool Alizee-bodied Volvo B12B 46 (YSU 914), seen here on a private hire duty, was new to Kenzies, Shepreth, in May 2005 registered K40 CBK. (Just Travel)

Resting in Tower Street, York, on 3 September 2019 while operating a park & ride duty for which it is branded, is First York Mercedes-Benz 0530G bendibus 11104 (BG58 OLV), which was new in January 2009. (K. A. Jenkinson)

Route branded for the 42 service from York to Drax and sporting a York & Country fleet name is Transdev Yorkshire Coastliner 727 (YX18 KZG), an Alexander Dennis E20D which began life in June 2018. (Author's collection)

Arriva Yorkshire North Wrightbus Gemini 3 1501 (YJ59 BTU) is seen here entering Piccadilly, York, on 3 September 2019 after being refurbished and given Arriva Sapphire livery together with branding for the 415 service to Selby. (K. A. Jenkinson)

Seen opposite York railway station while operating the Poppleton Bar park & ride service on 3 September 2019 is First York all-electric Optare VersaEV 49907 (YJ15 AYP), which was four and a half years old. (K. A. Jenkinson)

Displaying a York & Country fleet name and caught passing Clifford's Tower on 3 September 2019 is Transdev Yorkshire Coastliner Optare Versa 213 (YJ12 MZW), which had started life with Harrogate & District in April 2012. (K. A. Jenkinson)

With its passengers boarding, Transdev Yorkshire Coastliner's one-year-old Wrightbus Gemini 3 Stealth-bodied Volvo B5TL 3642 (BN68 XPR) is seen at York railway station on 3 September 2019. (K. A. Jenkinson)

New to First PMT in August 2005 but later owned by Stagecoach Merseyside and South Lancashire, Harrogate Coach Travel's (Connexionsbuses) immaculately presented Wrightbus Solar-bodied Scania L94UB YN05 WKF is seen here opposite York railway station on 3 September 2019 displaying branding for route 13. (K. A. Jenkinson)

Painted in a promotional livery for contactless payment of bus fares, First York Wrightbus Eclipse Gemini 2-bodied Volvo B9TL 37069 (YK57 EZZ) collects a solitary passenger opposite York railway station on 3 September 2019. (K. A. Jenkinson)

Standing outside York station on 3 September 2019, and branded for the X46 service to Hull, is East Yorkshire Alexander Dennis E40D 795 (YY64 GWX), which began life in November 2014 as a demonstrator for its manufacturer. (K. A. Jenkinson)

New to Lothian Buses in November 1999 but converted to open top in 2009, Plaxton-bodied Dennis Trident V519 ESC entered service with Transdev Yorkshire Coastliner in April 2017, numbered 4019. Here it is seen near York railway station on 3 September 2019, painted in City Sightseeing livery for the York Tour. (K. A. Jenkinson)

A few days after being transferred to First York from First Manchester, whose fleet name had been removed but can still be faintly seen on its side panels, Wrightbus Eclipse Gemini-bodied Volvo B9TL 37387 (MX58 DWW), which was new in September 2008, departs from York railway station on a city service on 3 September 2019. (K. A. Jenkinson)

Purchased new in September 2017, Connexionsbuses' twenty-one-seat Optare SoloSR YJ67 GGO is seen here on 3 September 2019 operating the local 16 service to Acomb. (K. A. Jenkinson)

Repainted into a Rider York heritage livery, First York's Wrightbus Eclipse Urban-bodied Volvo B7RLE 69374 (YJ08 XYO), which was new in August 2008, heads to Ashley Park on city service 11 on 3 September 2019. (K. A. Jenkinson)

Wearing a dedicated livery for the service to the University of York, First York Wrightbus Eclipse Gemini 2-bodied Volvo B9TL 37068 (YK57 EZX) is seen here opposite York railway station on 3 September 2019. (K. A. Jenkinson)

New to Harrogate & District in March 2004 registered YC53 MXY, and later refurbished and re-registered X10VTD, dual-purpose-seated Wrightbus Eclipse Gemini-bodied Volvo B7TL 3610 was transferred to Transdev Yorkshire Coastliner in 2016 and re-registered yet again to become LK02 ZAP. Here it is seen opposite York railway station on 3 September 2019, painted in the CityZap livery for operation on the express service to Leeds. (K. A. Jenkinson)

First York Wrightbus Eclipse Urban-bodied Volvo B7RLE 69279 (YJ57 YSR), with retrofitted roof edge advert panel, passes First York Mercedes-Benz 0530G bendibus 11104 (BG58 OLV) in Tower Street, York, on 3 September 2019. (K. A. Jenkinson)

Heading along Bridge Street, York, on 3 September 2019, is First York Wrightbus Eclipse Urban-bodied Volvo B7RLE 69363 (YJ08 XYB) painted in a promotional livery for tap and go fare payment. (K. A. Jenkinson)

Awaiting its Ghostbustours passengers alongside Clifford's Tower, York, is London Necrobus ex-London Iveco-engined AEC Routemaster KFF367, which was originally registered 101CLT when new. (T. M. Leach collection)

Seen in Nessgate, York, on 3 September 2019 is First York's electric-powered Optare VersaEV 49912 (YJ15 AYO), which is painted in a dedicated livery for the services to the university. (K. A. Jenkinson)

Seen in St Denys Road, York, on 3 September 2019, on the 36 service to Sutton-on-Derwent, for which it is branded, is York Pullman MCV-bodied Volvo B8RLE BV17 CPU, which was purchased new by its owner in May 2017. (K. A. Jenkinson)

Also seen in Piccadilly, York, on 3 September 2019, wearing its owner East Yorkshire's new livery, is MCV-bodied Volvo B5TL 793 (BP15 OLH), which was new in July 2015. (K. A. Jenkinson)

Passing along Piccadilly, York, on 3 September 2019 when only a few days old, is Transdev Yorkshire Coastliner's York and County-liveried Alexander Dennis E20D 755 (YW19 VUL). (K. A. Jenkinson)

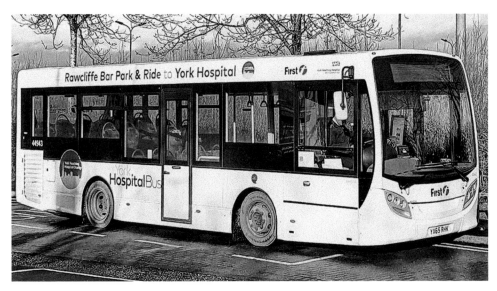

New to Reays, Wigton, in September 2015, Alexander Dennis E20D YX65 RHK is seen here in December 2019 after being acquired by First York who has numbered it 44943 and added York Hospital Bus branding for its dedicated operation on the service from Rawcliffe Bar park & ride site. (Tommy Holland)

All-electric Optare Metrodecker EV demonstrator YJ19 JCO is seen here at Poppleton Bar, York, in August 2019 while being trialled on the park & ride service upon which similar new buses are to be introduced in 2020. (Tommy Holland)

Seen at Monks Cross, York, in October 2019, a few days after its transfer to First York from First Manchester, is Wrightbus StreetLite DF 47479 (SN14 EAX). (Tommy Holland)

Starting life with Metroline London Northern in January 2001, Plaxton-bodied Volvo B7TL X636 LLX is seen here with Tockwith-based A&A Coach Travel after being converted to single-door layout. (Tommy Holland)

Climbing Station Rise, York, on 23 December 2019 on trade plates, and painted in the city's new park & ride livery, is the first of twenty-one all-electric Optare Metrodeckers purchased by First York for operation on the city's park & ride services. (First York/Richard Walker)